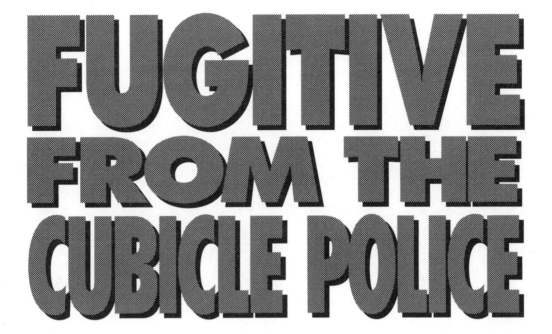

FUGITIVE FROM THE CUBICLE POLICE

A DILBERT™ BOOK BY SCOTT ADAMS

Andrews and McMeel
A Universal Press Syndicate Company
Kansas City

For Pam and the Cats.

Other Dilbert Books from Andrews and McMeel

Still Pumped from Using the Mouse
ISBN: 0-8362-1026-3

It's Obvious You Won't Survive by Your Wits Alone
ISBN: 0-8362-0415-8

Bring Me the Head of Willy the Mailboy!
ISBN: 0-8362-1779-9

Shave the Whales
ISBN: 0-8362-1740-3

Dogbert's Clues for the Clueless
ISBN: 0-8362-1737-3

Build a Better Life by Stealing Office Supplies
ISBN: 0-8362-1757-8

Always Postpone Meetings with Time-Wasting Morons
ISBN: 0-8362-1758-6

For ordering information, call 1-800-642-6480.

Introduction

I was doing some thinking today. But I didn't enjoy it very much, so I decided to write this introduction instead.

It seems as though every time I turn around, well, I get dizzy. So I stopped doing that. Now I only walk straight forward and backward and it has made my life much simpler. Granted, sometimes I have to tunnel through sheetrock, which is hard on my teeth. And my annoying neighbors are starting to whine about the holes in their houses. And it can take a VERY long time to get where I'm going, given the circumference of the earth and the hassle with immigration.

But when it starts to get me down I remember the story about the tortoise and his hair. If I recall, the tortoise had hair that grew very quickly. For some reason this was a problem. The tortoise eventually triumphed by beating his hair with his flipper.

Now you might say that tortoises (torti to be proper) do not have flippers. But if that's true, how could they fly? Or you might say that torti do indeed have flippers—I'm not really doing a whole lot of research for this part of the book—in which case, shut up.

And this brings me to my main point: I've been spending far too much time alone in my house since I became a cartoonist. My friends told me that the isolation, combined with my newfound prosperity, would have a negative impact on my mental state. So I paid a guy to kill them.

I'm kidding. I don't have friends. At least not good ones.

But if you'd like to be my friend—and Lord knows that's a hot ticket—you can do that by joining Dogbert's New Ruling Class.

As you might already know, when Dogbert conquers the planet and becomes supreme ruler, everyone who subscribes to the free Dilbert Newsletter will form the New Ruling Class and have complete dominion over everyone else. The others (we call them induhviduals) will be our domestic servants. Don't let that happen to you.

The Dilbert newsletter is free and it's published approximately "whenever I feel like it," which is about four times a year. There's an e-mail version and a snail mail version. The e-mail version is better.

E-mail subscription (preferred): write to scottadams@aol.com

Snail mail:

Dilbert Mailing List
c/o United Media
200 Madison Avenue
New York, NY 10016

S. Adams

http://www.unitedmedia.com/comics/dilbert

HAVE I TOLD YOU RECENTLY THAT I HAVE A LUCRATIVE JOB OFFER FROM OUR COMPETITOR?

YES

9-28

THE PAY IS OBSCENE, THEY WEAR CASUAL CLOTHES AT WORK, AND WEDNESDAY THROUGH FRIDAY IS FREE BEER AND PIZZA.

© 1993 United Feature Syndicate, Inc.

AS THE NEW GUY I GET TO DATE THE MASSEUSE UNTIL THE COMPANY MATCHES ME WITH AN ATTRACTIVE CO-WORKER.

SOB

NEXT WEEK I'LL BE AT MY NEW JOB, REAPING HUGE REWARDS.

WE'RE SO HAPPY FOR YOU.

9-29

BUT I'LL STILL HAVE A LITTLE CUBICLE LIKE YOURS.

© 1993 United Feature Syndicate, Inc.

THE ONLY DIFFERENCE BEING THAT I'LL KEEP A PONY THERE. THAT WAY IT'S CLOSE TO MY OFFICE.

14

36

42

44

58

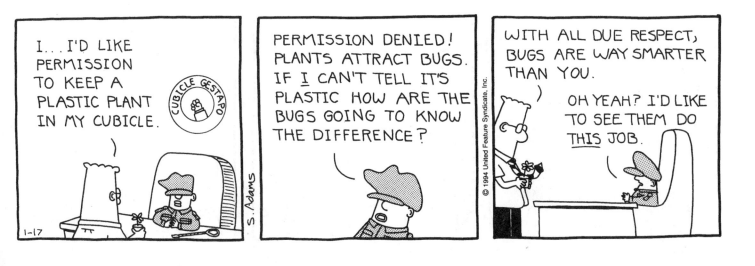

60

63

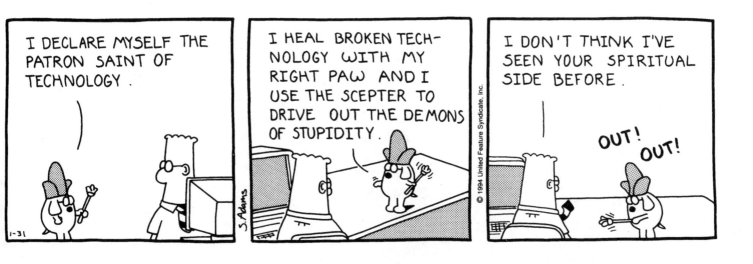

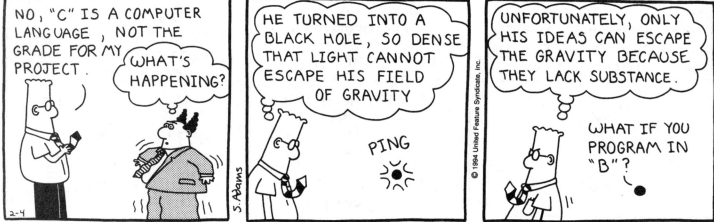

67

70

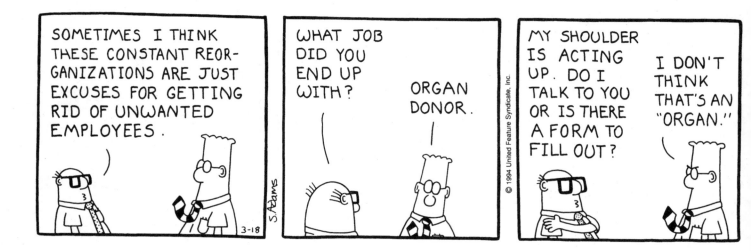

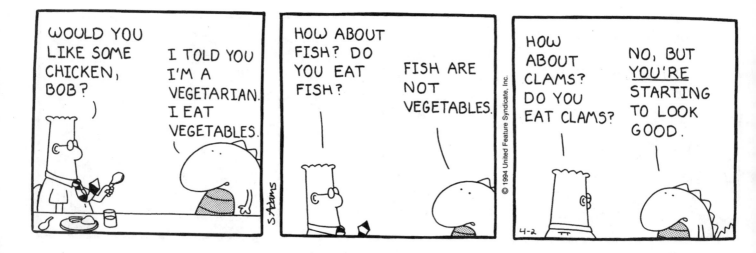

95

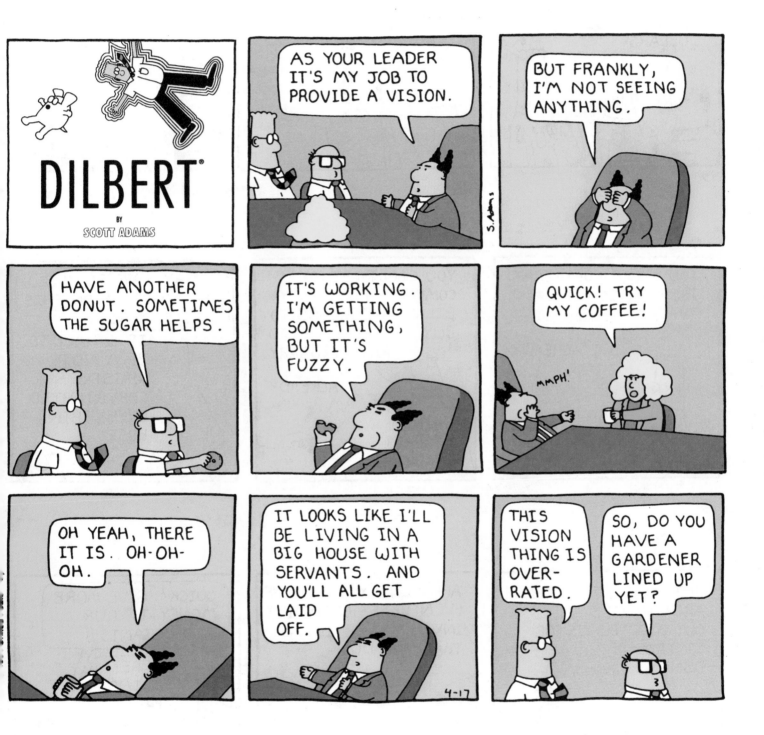

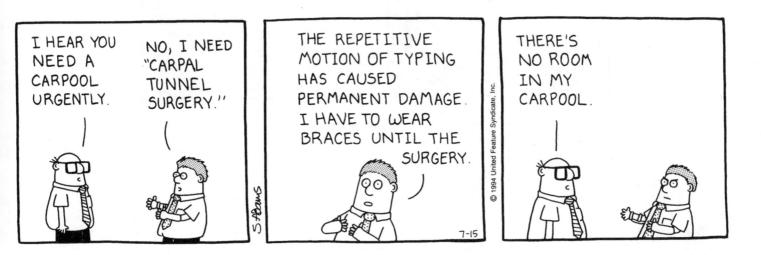

141

143

189

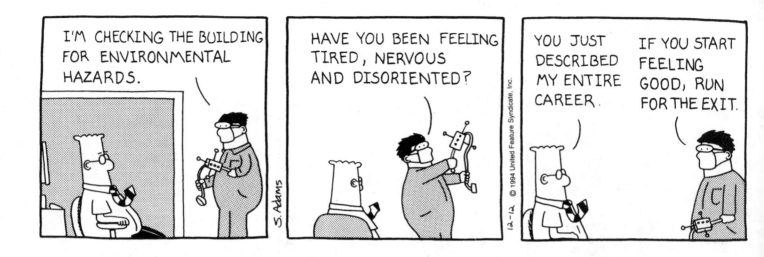